Who Is
Dolly Parton?

Who Is
Dolly Parton?

by True Kelley

illustrated by Stephen Marchesi

Penguin Workshop
An Imprint of Penguin Random House

For Jada, Jamaica, and Jessamine—TK

For Mercy Baron and the promise of a new day—SM

PENGUIN WORKSHOP
Penguin Young Readers Group
An Imprint of Penguin Random House LLC

Text copyright © 2014, 2017 by True Kelley. Illustrations copyright © 2014 by Stephen Marchesi. Cover illustration copyright © 2014 by Penguin Random House LLC. All rights reserved. Published by Penguin Workshop, an imprint of Penguin Random House LLC, 345 Hudson Street, New York, New York 10014. PENGUIN and PENGUIN WORKSHOP are trademarks of Penguin Books Ltd. WHO HQ & Design is a registered trademark of Penguin Random House LLC. Printed in the USA.

Library of Congress Control Number: 2014936899

ISBN 9780448478920   10 9 8 7

Contents

Who Is
Dolly Parton?

In Knoxville, Tennessee, in 1956, a tiny
girl with freckles stood alone and stared at the
microphone. She was about to sing on the radio
for the first time. She glanced at her Uncle Bill
offstage and then looked out at the crowd. She
was scared. All those eyes staring at her. Was a
shy ten-year-old country girl ready for this? There

were so many people here, and thousands more would be listening on their radios. It was her dream to do this, but now she wanted to run off the stage. Still, she knew this might be her only chance. She also knew her family was counting on her.

She took a shaky breath and began to sing. Her voice was thin and wobbly. Slowly it grew stronger. Soon, she was belting out her song. Almost before she finished, the crowd began cheering and clapping! They loved her! They loved her singing! They wanted more!

From that moment, Dolly Parton wanted more, too. She wanted to be a star. *Dream big, and big things can happen.* Those words would guide her throughout her life.

Even though she is only about five feet tall, Dolly stands out in any crowd with her curvy figure, glittery clothes, and big blond wigs. Dolly likes how she looks. She doesn't care what other

people think. She has always been true to herself.
Her upbeat, down-home, honest, and funny
personality charms everyone.

    There is no one else like her.

Chapter 1
The Parton Family

Dolly grew up in a large, poor family in Tennessee. Avie Lee Owens and Robert Lee Parton, Dolly's parents, married in 1939 when

Avie Lee was only fifteen and Lee was seventeen.
They rented a log cabin far out in the woods.
Avie Lee hated it and moved back with her
parents. There, she had her first baby, Willadeene.
After a year, Avie Lee and Lee got back together.
They moved into a rented shack in the foothills
of the Smoky Mountains. Lee was a hardworking
farmer. He grew tobacco, beans, corn, potatoes,
and turnips. But he was a sharecropper.

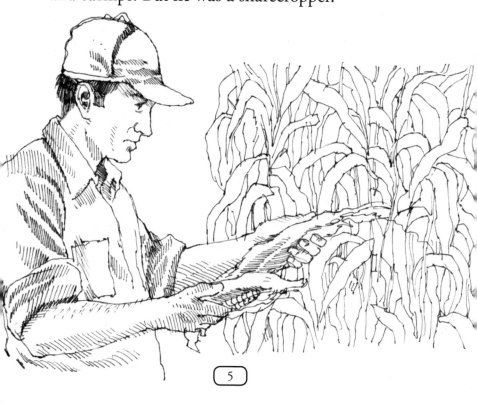

Sharecropping meant that Dolly's dad didn't own the land and had to share about half of the money from his crops with the landowner. It was a hard way to support a family, and soon another baby, David, came along . . . and then another, Denver.

By now, the five Partons had moved to a one-room cabin on the banks of the Little Pigeon River in East Tennessee. They didn't have electricity, running water, or an indoor bathroom.

One snowy winter
night, someone went to get
the doctor.

Avie Lee's fourth baby
was on the way. Doc
Thomas rode on horseback
to the cabin where Dolly
Parton was born on

January 19, 1946. The
Partons had no money, so they paid the doctor
with a bag of cornmeal. That was a good trade.

While Dolly was growing up, the Parton

family moved several times.
Once, they lived so far out
in the woods that their
nearest neighbors were two
miles away! The Partons had
no radio, newspapers, or
TV. They counted on their
neighbors for news and for

help in tough times. To go visiting, to church, or to school, they had to cross a river on a rope bridge and walk.

When Dolly was four, the Partons bought a farm. It was rundown, but it was theirs. They stayed there until Dolly was ten. Three or four Parton kids slept in one bed with all their clothes on.

THE GREAT SMOKY MOUNTAINS

KNOXVILLE o
SEVIERVILLE o
LITTLE PIGEON RIVER o

TENNESSEE

GREAT SMOKY MOUNTAINS

THE SMOKIES ARE PART OF THE APPALACHIAN MOUNTAIN RANGE. THEY ARE NAMED FOR THE FOG THAT OFTEN HANGS OVER THEM. THEY RUN ALONG THE TENNESSEE-NORTH CAROLINA BORDER IN THE SOUTHEASTERN UNITED STATES. THE HIGHEST PEAK IS CLINGMANS DOME AT 6,643 FEET.

CHEROKEE INDIANS LIVED IN THE FORESTS AND FOOTHILLS OF THE SMOKIES UNTIL SETTLERS FROM EUROPE FORCED THEM OUT. MANY OF THE SETTLERS WERE SCOTCH-IRISH. THEY LIVED

NORTH
CAROLINA

IN SIMPLE LOG CABINS AND FARMED IN THE
MOUNTAIN VALLEYS. MUSIC AND RELIGION WERE
VERY IMPORTANT AND HELPED BRING ISOLATED
COUNTRY PEOPLE TOGETHER.

FROM THE DEPRESSION THROUGH THE 1950S,
THE AREA WAS DESPERATELY POOR. PEOPLE
STARTED TO LEAVE BECAUSE THERE WERE SO
FEW JOBS. TODAY, TOURISM HAS HELPED THE
AREA WITH ATTRACTIONS LIKE THE GREAT SMOKY
MOUNTAINS NATIONAL PARK AND DOLLYWOOD.

The cabin walls were covered with newspapers
instead of wallpaper. Dolly liked to read the walls!
Dolly said later that they had "two rooms and a
path and running water, if you were willing to run
to get it." She meant that the kids had to run and
fetch water from outside. They couldn't just go to
a sink and turn on a faucet.

Lee did all he
could to keep
his family fed.
He fished and
hunted, and everyone ate what
nature provided: rabbit,
squirrel, groundhog,
turtle, or bear. He
grew vegetables and
kept bees. Almost
the only foods they
bought were coffee
and sugar.

Avie Lee worked
really hard, too,

canning, pickling, making clothes, and caring
for the children. She was often sick; her hard life
was wearing her down. She almost died giving

birth to her next child, and the baby, little Larry, did not make it. Losing Larry was terribly sad for everyone, but especially Dolly. Dolly sat by Larry's grave for hours. Her mother had said that Larry would be Dolly's special baby to care for. It was a custom in big families for an older child to take special care of one of the younger ones. Dolly had been her big sister Willadeene's special baby.

The only toys that the Parton kids had were homemade. Lee made wooden wagons and cardboard-box sleds. Avie Lee made paper dolls and dollhouses and trains from old oatmeal boxes and matchboxes and spools. Dolly's mom once made her a corncob doll called "Tiny Tassel Top." People said that Dolly's first song was about her. When Dolly was five, Avie Lee wrote

APPALACHIAN MOUNTAIN MUSIC

APPALACHIAN MUSIC IS STORYTELLING MUSIC. WHENEVER PEOPLE GOT TOGETHER, THEY PLAYED MUSIC AND SANG ABOUT THEIR OWN LIVES AND PROBLEMS. THE SONGS TOLD OF LONELINESS, HARDSHIP, SADNESS, RELIGION, AND LOST LOVE. DOLLY WROTE AND SANG MANY OF THESE KINDS OF SONGS, SUCH AS "JOSHUA," A SONG ABOUT A LONELY MAN AND WOMAN WHO FIND LOVE.

down one of Dolly's songs. It was an unusual song for a little girl to sing. The title was, "Life Doesn't Mean That Much to Me"!

Many of Dolly's relatives loved music. Her grandfather was a preacher, who also taught and wrote music. Dolly's great grandmother played an instrument called the dulcimer and made up songs. She sang old Irish- and British-style folk songs. Music was a big part of life for the people of the Smoky Mountains.

Early on, everyone in Dolly's family noticed how musical she was. Her grandfather Jake said Dolly "started singing as soon as she quit crying." She also loved singing with her sisters in church. Dolly sometimes forced her sisters Stella and Cassie to sing back-up to songs she had made up. Dolly put a tin can on a stick and pretended it was a microphone. The porch was a stage. She put on shows for the chickens and any of her brothers and sisters she could trap. Her biggest dream was to be on the Grand Ole Opry, the famous country music radio show.

Already, little Dolly dreamed big.

GRAND OLE OPRY

JOHNNY CASH

THE GRAND OLE OPRY IS A RADIO SHOW IN NASHVILLE. IT PLAYS BLUEGRASS, FOLK, COUNTRY, GOSPEL, AND COUNTRY ROCK. SINCE 1925, PEOPLE IN MOST OF THE UNITED STATES AND PARTS OF CANADA HAVE LISTENED TO IT EVERY WEEK. THE SHOW IS STILL PUT ON LIVE EVERY WEEK ON RADIO AND TV. TOP COUNTRY STARS PERFORM. MANY GOT THEIR START ON THE SHOW: LEGENDS LIKE PATSY CLINE, HANK WILLIAMS, AND JOHNNY CASH. TODAY, TOP OPRY STARS INCLUDE DOLLY PARTON, REBA MCENTIRE, CARRIE UNDERWOOD, GARTH BROOKS, AND RASCAL FLATTS.

Chapter 2
Country Roots

Dolly's parents didn't have much time for their kids. They worked so hard just to survive. It was a struggle to buy new shoes each year for twelve children.

The Parton kids invented their own fun. Dolly remembers tying June bugs to a string and calling them "'lectric kites." The kids were outdoors all the time. They ran barefoot all summer. Dolly

was a tomboy. Once Dolly jumped over a fence
and cut her foot so badly her toes were barely
hanging on. Avie Lee sewed them back on, and
they healed fine.

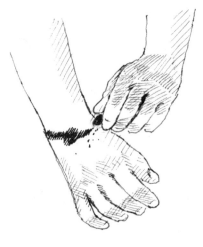

The Parton girls used purple pokeberries to paint bracelets and wristwatches on their arms. They painted what they called "Jesus sandals" on their feet and pretended to be people from the Bible. Dolly wanted to work in a beauty salon. Pokeberries made good lipstick. Her mother didn't always approve!

Dolly knew she did not want to stay on the farm. She hated working in the fields. Dolly thought of an escape plan. She got her brothers

and sisters to help her dig a hole. For months they
kept on digging. Dolly's plan was to dig all the
way to China!

DOLLY'S BROTHERS AND SISTERS

MOST OF DOLLY'S BROTHERS AND SISTERS ARE
CREATIVE AND MUSICAL. STELLA, RANDY, FLOYD,
FRIEDA, AND RACHEL ARE ALL PERFORMERS AND
SONGWRITERS. WILLADEENE IS AN AUTHOR AND
POET. DOLLY SAID SHE'S LIKE A SECOND MOTHER
TO ALL HER BROTHERS AND SISTERS. CASSIE
WORKS FOR DOLLY, MANAGING HER PROPERTIES.
BOBBY AND DAVID ARE BOTH BUILDERS. DENVER,
A FARMER, NAMED HIS FIRST DAUGHTER AFTER
DOLLY.

Dolly and her brothers and sisters walked two miles to school every day. The school had eight grades and only fifteen students. Most of them were Partons! Dolly met seven-year-old Judy Ogle there. They became best friends for life. Judy wrote down Dolly's songs for her. (Dolly never learned to read music.) Judy still helps Dolly today. They have been best friends for over fifty-five years!

Dolly hated school. She was too fidgety to sit quietly at her desk. She'd bang her heels on the desk just to make noise. She got up to sharpen her pencil a thousand times a day. She was the class clown. She was always being punished.

Even though she hated school, Dolly loved to read. Fairy tales were her favorite, but she read everything she could get her hands on: catalogs, the *Farmer's Almanac*, the Bible, and even the funeral-home directory!

One day, when Dolly was nine, the school burned down! Luckily, nobody was inside at the time. But it meant that Dolly had to go to a bigger school farther away. There were richer kids at the new school. They looked down their noses at the

Partons. They called Dolly "Rag Top." She was embarrassed to be so poor, but she never let it show.

One morning the teacher asked the kids to each tell what they had for breakfast. One by one, they listed fruit juices, bacon and eggs, cereal and toast. Dolly never had more than plain biscuits and gravy, and she knew the others would make fun of that. So when her turn came she made up a big fancy breakfast of eggs, bacon, oatmeal, orange juice, and toast. Then she started to worry. Her brother Denver was in the same class. And Denver never lied! What would he say? When it was his turn, Denver just looked hard at his sister and said, "I had the same thing Dolly had."

When Dolly needed a new winter coat, her mom made one out of scraps of cloth. The coat had so many beautiful colors! Dolly knew how much love her mother had put into sewing it. It was the most gorgeous coat Dolly had ever seen.

She couldn't wait to wear it to school. But when she did, the other kids made fun of her. Dolly was crushed. Years later she wrote a children's book and a song about it. "The Coat of Many Colors" is still Dolly's favorite song. Her dad cried when he first heard it.

Chapter 3
Radio Days

No matter what the kids at school thought, Dolly's family was always proud of her. They saw that she was special and talented, and they did a lot to help her succeed.

Uncle Louis noticed Dolly singing all the time and playing a guitar she had made for herself. When she was about eight, he gave her a guitar.

It was an old one, but it was real.

Dolly's uncle Bill Owens was a musician. He wanted to help Dolly, too. He got her a chance to sing on the Cas Walker Radio Show, in Knoxville, Tennessee, forty miles away. Dolly had wanted to be on that show since going there on a class field trip.

BILL OWENS

Cas Walker watched the small ten-year-old stand up to the microphone and sing a church song. The audience loved her. Cas hired her on the spot! Dolly sang on the show on Saturdays, during vacations, and all summer. Sometimes she even skipped school to perform.

Soon Cas Walker also had a TV show, and Dolly got to be on it. But Dolly's family couldn't watch her, because they didn't have a TV. Once,

Cas Walker did a
publicity stunt before
his show. He dared
people to climb a fifty-
foot pole to get a fifty-
dollar bill at the top.
The pole had grease on
it and was very slippery.
No one could do it.
Dolly had an idea. After
she got herself all wet, she
rolled around in sand. Then
she scooted right up the pole
and grabbed the money! It
was enough to buy her family
a TV!

What would Dolly have
done without her family?
Uncle Bill drove Dolly to
her shows. Uncle Louis took

Dolly to make tapes of her songs and sent them to record companies and the Grand Ole Opry.

Uncle Bill helped Dolly to write a song, "Puppy Love." Another uncle, John Henry, paid for Dolly and her grandmother to go to Louisiana so Dolly could record the song in a studio there. It was

the first time either of them had ever been out of Tennessee. It was a hard trip. They missed a bus in Alabama. What would they do now? They didn't even have money for food. Somehow Dolly and her grandma got to the studio and back, and the record was made.

THE CAS WALKER RADIO SHOW

CAS WALKER STARTED THE RADIO SHOW TO ADVERTISE HIS GROCERY STORES. HE HIRED MANY WELL-KNOWN COUNTRY, GOSPEL, AND BLUEGRASS MUSICIANS TO PERFORM IN PERSON. THE EVERLY BROTHERS, WHO WERE TEENAGED STARS, WERE OFTEN ON THE SHOW IN THE MID-1950S. THAT MUST HAVE MADE DOLLY WANT TO BE ON THE SHOW EVEN MORE.

Dolly was still singing on the Cas Walker Show. She was only thirteen when she moved in with her Aunt Estelle near Knoxville to be closer to the show.

Uncle Bill took Dolly to Nashville to try to get her on the Grand Ole Opry. It was almost impossible because she was so young. Backstage before the show, Uncle Bill begged the performers to let Dolly go on. One of them let Dolly take his place. This was Dolly's biggest break so far! The famous singing star Johnny Cash introduced

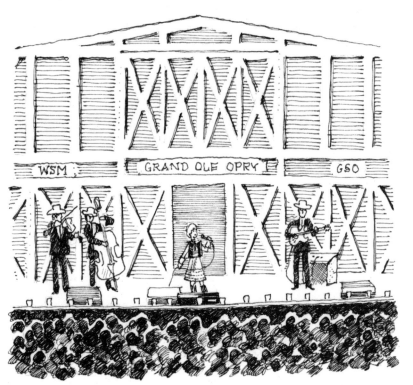

Dolly, and she sang "You Gotta Be My Baby."
Four thousand people were there. She had three
encores! Dolly's dreams were coming true!

Uncle Bill and Dolly made more trips to
Nashville. They wrote songs together for a music
company. They made a record for Mercury
Records in 1962, but it didn't do that well. They
were barely making enough money to get by.

Dolly wanted to go home to graduate from high school just to show she could. Dolly still hated school. She wasn't popular and was shy around boys. Dolly thought she was ugly and needed lots of makeup and powder. She was barely five feet tall. To look taller she teased her bleached hair to be the biggest hair in school. She liked to look like a showgirl. But the other girls thought she looked trashy.

Dolly's love of music helped her survive. Dolly and Judy Ogle, still her best friend, played drums in the marching band. They wrote songs together during drum practice.

In 1964, Dolly graduated from Sevier County
High School. She was the first in her family to get a
high-school diploma. They were very proud of her.

After the graduation, her classmates all met and

announced their plans for the future. Dolly stood
and said, "I'm going to Nashville, and I'm gonna
be a star."

All her classmates burst out laughing.

Chapter 4
Nashville

The day after graduation, eighteen-year-old Dolly said good-bye to her family and got on the bus to Nashville. She carried paper bags full of her stuff and a bag of biscuits. She cried for the whole two-hundred-mile trip.

WHY GO TO NASHVILLE?

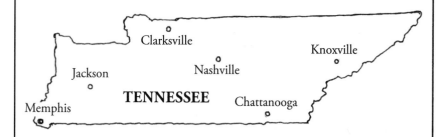

NASHVILLE IS THE CAPITAL OF TENNESSEE, BUT IT'S MOST FAMOUS AS A CENTER FOR COUNTRY MUSIC. IT IS HOME TO THE GRAND OLE OPRY. ONE PART OF THE CITY, CALLED MUSIC ROW, HAS HUNDREDS OF COUNTRY, GOSPEL, AND CHRISTIAN MUSIC COMPANIES. IT HAS RECORDING STUDIOS, MUSIC PUBLISHERS, LABELS, AND RADIO STATIONS. THERE ARE MANY CLUBS AND PLACES TO HEAR AND PLAY MUSIC. THE COUNTRY MUSIC HALL OF FAME AND MUSEUM IS THERE, AND THE COUNTRY MUSIC AWARDS MUSIC FESTIVAL IS HELD THERE EVERY YEAR.

Dolly moved in with her Uncle Bill and his wife and baby until she could get work and find a place of her own. On her first day in Nashville, Dolly was waiting for her laundry in front of the Wishy-Washy Laundromat when a handsome stranger called out to her, "Y'all gonna get sunburnt out there, little lady." Dolly was such a

country girl, she didn't know she shouldn't speak to strangers. That was how she met Carl Dean, her future husband. They started dating, but then Carl joined the army and was away for two years. Dolly's best friend Judy was away in the air force. Dolly was terribly lonely and homesick.

CARL DEAN

Meanwhile, Uncle Bill helped Dolly meet more people in the music business. Every day Dolly knocked on doors and tried to give away tapes of her songs. No luck.

She took waitress and office jobs to get by. Dolly finally got work singing on a local TV show at 5:00 a.m. every morning. It paid enough for her to rent her own place. But Dolly had hardly any money left over for food. Sometimes she ate

ketchup, mustard, and water soup. Dolly was
so hungry that she went into hotels and took
leftovers from trays that people had put in the
halls. On a visit home everyone was shocked how
skinny she was.

Dolly and Uncle Bill headed out in his old
station wagon to find places where they could

perform. They often slept in the car—Uncle Bill in front and Dolly in back. They played in bars . . . some places had chicken wire to protect performers from things thrown by the audience. Dolly was exhausted but still managed to write songs every day. She wrote over one hundred songs in three years (some of them with Bill). Dolly didn't just write love songs. She wrote about the ups and downs of country life: motherhood, children, mental illness, poverty, birth, and death.

Less than two years after high school, Dolly
got to record with Bill for Monument Records, an
important record label in Nashville. Their records
didn't do well, but Dolly was asked to appear on a
TV show, *Chicago Bandstand*. Dolly flew there. It
was her first time on an airplane. Dolly hated it.

She never wanted to fly again! She still doesn't like it today.

Slowly Dolly was learning the business end of music, as well as writing and performing. Famous country singers Hank Williams Jr. and Kitty Wells recorded two of Dolly's songs. Dolly sang back-up on a hit record for a well-known singer named Bill Phillips. Her name wasn't on the label. People wondered who had the clear 'mystery voice.' People were starting to notice Dolly!

In 1965, Carl got back from the army. He and Dolly were still in love. They wanted to get married. Dolly's record company thought it was a bad idea because she might lose fans if she had a husband. So Dolly and Carl got married secretly on May 30, 1966, in Ringgold, Georgia.

Carl has always been a very private man. Unlike Dolly, he doesn't like being in the spotlight. In fact, he has rarely even seen Dolly perform. Carl ran a road-paving business in

Nashville. Dolly was busy with her career and was often away from home. So they couldn't spend much time together. Most couples don't live this way. Gossip newspapers have always found their marriage very interesting! However, Dolly and Carl have been together for over forty-five years. Dolly says, "We're really proud of our marriage. It's the first for both of us. And the last."

Chapter 5
A Star Is Born

In 1967, very few country music stars were women. Dolly was ready to fill the gap!

Porter Wagoner, a country-music entertainer, had a very successful TV show. His girl singer, Norma Jean, left to get married. So Porter needed a new singer. Dolly and about twenty others tried out for the job. Porter liked Dolly's personality, and he hired her!

THE PORTER WAGONER SHOW

FROM 1960 TO 1981, PORTER WAGONER TOURED THE UNITED STATES BY BUS FROM TOWN TO TOWN WITH HIS TV COUNTRY VARIETY SHOW. PEOPLE LOVED THE COUNTRY MUSIC AND CORNY JOKES. PORTER DRESSED IN FLASHY CLOTHES. HE HAD PINK AND PURPLE SUITS COVERED WITH RHINESTONES.

PORTER AND HIS BAND, THE WAGONMASTERS, ENTERTAINED OVER THREE MILLION VIEWERS. HE SANG DUETS WITH HIS "GAL SINGER" NORMA JEAN, UNTIL DOLLY REPLACED HER.

At first, Porter's audience was upset. They missed Norma Jean. They heckled Dolly, and she left the stage in tears. Dolly suffered for six months, but she stuck it out. Over time, the audience grew to love her. She ended up working with  Porter for seven years. She later said it was the hardest and worst period of her life. But she also said those years were the most "productive and growth-filled ones."

Dolly did a hundred shows a year with Porter, plus recording sessions. They might tape two TV shows in an hour! Porter was hospitalized for stress more than once. Dolly got only a few hours sleep each night. Sometimes she slept in her makeup and wig so she could get back to work early the next morning. Even with this schedule, she kept writing songs. (Over the course of her career she has written over three thousand!)

Dolly learned a lot from Porter Wagoner. He taught her to be professional and to always look like a star. In 1967 Dolly recorded a duet with Porter for RCA Records. It was in the top ten country recordings. Thirteen more hit duets followed, and many awards. Dolly made enough

money to buy a Cadillac. It was a big, fancy car, and very exciting for a country girl! She had never had a car before and was a terrible driver . . . which made it even more exciting!

Then Dolly was asked to record an album without Porter. This was an amazing chance.

Dolly drove her new car to the recording studio . . . and crashed it into a brick wall in the studio parking lot! Dolly forgot to use the brakes! Luckily, she wasn't hurt. Bricks were still falling on the hood as Dolly strolled into the studio as if nothing had happened! After the recording was done, everyone left and saw the smashed Cadillac stuck in the wall. *What!?* Whose car was it? Dolly was too smart to let on that it was hers.

Now Dolly and Carl were able to buy a two-story house south of Nashville.

They were not able to have any children of their
own, but they took in five of her younger brothers
and sisters. They called Dolly "Aunt Granny."
Dolly's sister Stella took care of the kids while
Dolly worked to support everybody.

Only three years after she first went to Nashville, Dolly's hometown declared Dolly Parton Day. Seven thousand people in Sevierville came to a parade in her honor. Some of her high-school classmates must have been in the crowd. They didn't laugh at her now. Dolly was doing exactly what she said she would. She was becoming a star!

Dolly had a new hit album,  *Hello, I'm Dolly*. The song, "Dumb Blonde" was on that album. The words said, "'Cause this dumb blonde ain't nobody's fool." Dolly was talking about herself, because she certainly was 'nobody's fool.' In 1968 Dolly's album *Just Because I'm a Woman* was another hit. Dolly often sang about strong women.

Ideas for songs often came to Dolly at night. By morning she might have ten new songs! There were songs about memories, feelings, country life, and the hardships of being poor. She wrote songs about her own problems, too. She said as soon as she did, the problems went away! Dolly liked to sing tearjerker songs that could make people cry. One song, "Silver Sandals," was about a crippled girl who swaps her crutches for silver sandals so she can climb the golden stairs to heaven.

THE WOMEN'S MOVEMENT

BY THE 1960S, MANY WOMEN WERE NO LONGER
HAPPY ONLY BEING HOUSEWIVES AND MOTHERS.
THEY WANTED JOBS, JOBS THAT UP TO THAT
POINT HAD BEEN CONSIDERED MEN'S JOBS. WHY
COULDN'T MORE WOMEN BE DOCTORS, POLITICIANS,
ENGINEERS, OR SCIENTISTS . . . OR TRUCK
DRIVERS OR CARPENTERS OR POLICE OFFICERS?
WOMEN ALSO WANTED THE SAME PAY THAT MEN
GOT FOR DOING THE SAME JOB. THE WOMEN'S
MOVEMENT (ALSO KNOWN AS WOMEN'S LIBERATION
OR THE FEMINIST MOVEMENT) WORKED TO MAKE
ALL OF THIS HAPPEN. LAWS WERE PASSED TO
TREAT WOMEN FAIRLY, AND HEALTH CARE CHANGED
TO BETTER SERVE WOMEN'S NEEDS. TODAY, ALL OF
SOCIETY OWES MUCH TO THE WOMEN'S MOVEMENT.

At age twenty-three, Dolly's long-held dream
came true. She joined the cast of the Grand Ole
Opry! Porter and Dolly did more duet albums,
TV, and concerts. Porter also was Dolly's
manager. He had wanted her to become a star.
But now she was getting to be a bigger star than

he was! Songs that she wrote were more popular than his. That wasn't easy for Porter.

In 1971, Dolly had a number one country hit: "Joshua." It was a touching song about a lonely man and woman who fall in love. The same year Dolly sang "Coat of Many Colors" about the beautiful coat Avie Lee had made so long ago. In 1973, she had her biggest hit so far: "Jolene," about a beautiful woman who takes away someone else's sweetheart.

Things were happening fast. In one year, Dolly came out with five albums (two of them were duets with Porter). All were big hits. Suddenly, Dolly had money. Lots of money. She was able to buy her parents a house and her mother her first car.

Meanwhile, Dolly and Porter were not getting along. They fought and yelled at each other. Finally, they split up. Porter was bitter, but not Dolly. She was grateful to Porter for all that he had done. She wrote a song about him, "I Will Always Love You."

It was number one on the country charts.

Chapter 6
Bigger Dreams

SANDY GALLIN

Around 1976, Dolly found a new big-time Hollywood manager, Sandy Gallin. He managed stars like Cher. Dolly got an apartment in Los Angeles. Sandy thought she should branch out into pop music and not just do country music. He was right. Dolly soon had her first million-selling record, *Here You Come Again*. In 1979, it won a Grammy award for Best Country Female Vocal Performance! Winning a Grammy is as important to musicians

as winning an Oscar is
to actors. She also had
her own TV show,
Dolly, in the 1980s
and often appeared
on other TV shows
like *The Tonight
Show, Cher,* and
Hollywood Squares.
Dolly toured
in London, Sweden,
Alaska, and Hawaii. She
was working so hard, she lost her voice! Dolly had
to cancel a lot of shows, as well as her new TV
show, to rest her voice.

Dolly, Carl, and Dolly's five younger brothers
and sisters moved to a twenty-three-room mansion
outside Nashville. Carl, who was retired, helped
build it. Willow Lake Plantation was their dream
house with a swimming pool and a lot of land.

In 1977, Dolly formed a band called Gypsy Fever with some of her family. Since Dolly still hated to fly, the band went on tour in a very fancy bus called "The Coach of Many Colors." It was pink, purple, and silver on the outside. Inside, it was yellow, bright pink, and orange. There was a kitchen, a dining area, a shower with a tiny tub, a lounge, a private suite with a queen bed and prayer altar, and bunk beds for the driver and guests. The bus also had closets for wigs and costumes

DOLLY'S INSTRUMENTS

DOLLY DOESN'T JUST PLAY GUITAR. SHE CAN ALSO PLAY PIANO, BANJO, DRUMS, SAXOPHONE, RECORDER, AUTOHARP, BASS GUITAR, DULCIMER, FIDDLE, HARMONICA, AND PENNYWHISTLE. SHE TAUGHT HERSELF TO PLAY THEM ALL!

MANY OF THE INSTRUMENTS DOLLY PLAYS ARE OLD-TIME COUNTRY INSTRUMENTS.

THE DULCIMER IS AN INSTRUMENT THAT DOLLY'S GRANDMOTHER HAD PLAYED. IT HAS STRINGS LIKE A GUITAR AND IS PLAYED HELD FLAT ON THE LAP. IT'S ALSO CALLED A "HOG FIDDLE."

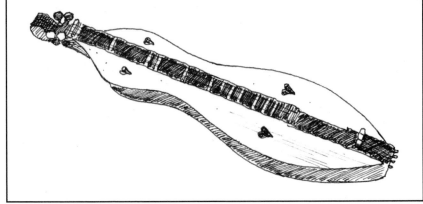

and a cosmetic area. Dolly liked staying in the bus much more than in fancy hotel rooms.

Dolly and Gypsy Fever had to fly, though, to perform in England. The British people loved Dolly. She even performed for and met Queen Elizabeth II of England. Dolly said that the queen wore "just as much jewelry as I did, though maybe she was a little tastier with it."

Even meeting the queen, Dolly wore a big blond wig and dressed as flashy as usual. Dolly liked herself the way she was. She joked, "It takes a lot of money to look this cheap!"

Dolly continued to put out many more big hits and collect many awards for her special mix of pop and country. She said, "I'm not leaving country. I'm just taking it with me." In 1978, she was named Country Music Association's Entertainer of the Year. She wasn't just a star; now she was a superstar!

Stardom came with problems. Porter Wagoner was unhappy that he wasn't getting a share of Dolly's success. He bad-mouthed her and sued her for a lot of money. There were battles in court which wore Dolly down. Gossip magazines were hard on her because she was gaining weight. Dolly loved her fried chicken . . . especially when she was under stress.

But Dolly still kept on dreaming. She was

a singing star. She was a TV star. What else
could she do? What about movies? What about
Hollywood?

Chapter 7
Hollywood Dolly

Dolly never thought of herself as a movie star, but she was offered a role she couldn't refuse . . . playing someone very much like herself! The famous actress Jane Fonda sent her a script for a movie that would be called *Nine to Five*. It was a comedy about three women who work for a terrible boss and how they get even with him. Dolly played a secretary, Doralee, who, at the end of the movie, becomes a country-western singer! On the first day, Dolly arrived at the film studio in Los Angeles with the entire script memorized . . . not just her own part. Everybody else's, too!

Dolly thought movie-making was fun, and she threw herself into it. Every day, she came to work

at 4:00 a.m. in full makeup and wig. Then a studio makeup artist would completely redo her makeup for the cameras. Dolly wrote a theme song for the movie on the back of her script. The song was also called "Nine to Five." When the movie came out in 1980, the song became number one on the pop and country charts. The movie was a box-office hit, too.

The next big movie Dolly made was not as much fun. Some of the other actors and the director were hard to work with. But for Dolly the biggest problem with making movies was all the waiting around. She had too much energy for that.

Even so, Dolly kept on the lookout for other movie roles. In 1989, she starred in another film with top actresses such as Shirley MacLaine and

Julia Roberts. *Steel Magnolias* was about a close group of friends who gather in a beauty shop in Louisiana. The women stick together through ups and downs. It's a funny movie but a tearjerker. Dolly actually learned to cut hair to prepare for her role as a hairdresser. Dolly said the part was exactly who she would have been if she had stayed home and had no singing career.

Other movies Dolly starred in include *Rhinestone* (1984), *Straight Talk* (1992), and *Joyful Noise* (2012) with the singer and actress Queen Latifah.

In 1980, Dolly signed a big contract to do shows for six weeks a year in Las Vegas, Nevada. Las Vegas hotels host flashy shows with major stars. Dolly's shows were spectacular in spite of voice trouble and weight problems.

Unfortunately, Dolly was trying to do too much. Her health was suffering, and she felt really low. She didn't even feel like playing her guitar or writing songs for months. She needed a vacation! Someplace quiet and far away . . . maybe Australia!

However, when she arrived in quiet, faraway Australia, Dolly was mobbed by screaming fans. To escape, she rented a little houseboat off a remote island. That sounded peaceful. However, her boat was caught in a huge storm. Dolly's

high heels were washed overboard, and Dolly almost went with them! The vacation was not a vacation at all. Dolly returned to the United States to do a thirty-five-show tour. She was overtired and often sick.

In 1982, Dolly ended up in the hospital for some minor surgery. She knew she had to learn to take better care of herself. But she just couldn't slow down.

Dolly made a very successful family movie for TV, *A Smoky Mountain Christmas* (1986). The story was sort of like *Snow White and the Seven Dwarfs*. But the story was also in part about Dolly herself. It told of a lonely, stressed-out singer who retreats to a log cabin in the mountains and finds seven orphans there. Dolly wrote many of the songs in the movie.

In 1988, Dolly had a new TV variety show on ABC, *Dolly*. It did well at first, but it seemed outdated. The jokes were a little too corny, and Dolly and her guests seemed as if they were trying too hard to have fun. The show was a disappointment to Dolly, except for the appearance of one very important guest: Porter Wagoner. Dolly and Porter had a wonderful TV

reunion. Dolly put aside their old arguments and treated him with all the respect due to the man who played such an important part in her career.

Of course, Dolly still was churning out hit pop songs. But now Dolly wanted to return to her roots in country music. She recorded an album of country and folk music with singers Emmylou Harris and Linda Ronstadt. It was called *Trio* and was nominated for the Album of the Year Grammy Award and won the Grammy Award for Best Country Performance by a Duo or Group with Vocal. Partly because that music was the kind she'd grown up with, Dolly said getting that Grammy was a high point in her life.

Chapter 8
Dollywood Dolly

Dolly Parton is talented in so many different ways. She is also a very smart businesswoman. People call her "the Iron Butterfly." That means she looks delicate but is tough. In 2004 *The Wall Street Journal* called her "one of the most important women in the world for business and industry."

Dolly runs a huge group of businesses called Dolly Parton Enterprises. She has had her own record, movie-production, and music-publishing companies. She even owns theme parks! She has invested in real estate, restaurants, dinner theaters, radio stations, farm equipment, hardware stores, garden centers, and macadamia nuts!

Dolly makes sensible and intelligent business

decisions. Many years ago, Elvis Presley wanted to buy the rights to her song, "I Will Always Love You." Elvis would have owned it. But Dolly said no. Since then she has made millions of dollars on just that one song. Many performers have recorded it. The version by Whitney Houston is the most famous. According to Dolly, that one has made so much money that Dolly could have bought Graceland, Elvis's home!

Of all her businesses, Dolly is proudest of Dollywood. That is her theme park in Pigeon Forge, Tennessee, near where she grew up. It's like a big country fair. There are merry-go-rounds, roller coasters, and bumper cars. There's a theater where some of Dolly's relatives perform. Nearby, people Dolly calls "skillbillies" demonstrate country skills like blacksmithing, weaving, glass-

blowing, and leather-working. There is even a
steam-powered saw mill and a life-size mountain
homestead. The Southern Gospel Hall of Fame is
there, too. Nearby is Dollywood's Splash Country,
Tennessee's largest water park, and Dolly's Dixie
Stampede, a dinner theater she touts "is the most
fun place to eat in the Smokies."

With over four million visitors a year, Dollywood

and Splash Country have created a lot of jobs for local people. Money from the parks helps fund the Dollywood Foundation. It is a charity that inspires kids to read and stay in school.

Dolly Parton never liked school much. But she understands the importance of a good education. In Sevier County, Tennessee, a lot of kids were dropping out of high school. Through the Dollywood Foundation, Dolly started giving students five-hundred dollars if they graduated. That cut the dropout rate in half. The Foundation also provided scholarships, computer labs for schools, and clothes and school supplies for needy kids.

Dolly had seen how not being able to read had held back her dad. In 1996, Dolly started her Imagination Library. It gave a book a month to every child in Sevier County

from birth to school age. Since then, more than 115 million books have been handed out in the United States, Canada, Australia, and the United Kingdom. Kids call Dolly "the Book Lady." She's proud to be known by that name. Then in 2009 she got an honorary doctorate from the University of Tennessee . . . so now she's also Dr. Dolly Parton!

Dolly has supported the Red Cross, HIV/AIDS charities, a hospital charity, and charities for animals like the American Eagle Foundation. She believes in the right of gay people to marry and says so, which caused her trouble with some fans. But Dolly puts her beliefs first. Her motto is "Dream more, learn more, care more, and be more."

Chapter 9
The Living Legend

The Living Legend Award from the Music City News had been given to many of Dolly's heroes like Johnny Cash and Tammy Wynette. In 1994, Dolly won it! That same year, while still making hit records, she published an autobiography, a children's book, and started her own recording label, Blue Eye Records! She worked with other stars, young and old such as Loretta Lynn, Neil Diamond, and Billy Ray Cyrus, whose daughter, Miley, is Dolly's god-daughter.

Dolly is never afraid to try something new. She has worked with non country artists like Rod Stewart, Elton John, and Norah Jones. She did an album of patriotic songs called *For God and Country.* She also did albums that included sixties hits like John Lennon's "Imagine." Dolly went back to her roots again and made very successful bluegrass albums. She even sang a bluegrass version of Carl's favorite Led Zeppelin song, "Stairway to Heaven," though Carl was honest and told her he didn't like it.

Between recording sessions, Dolly and Carl sometimes got away with their dog in a camper van, staying in motels and eating in diners. Dolly would go in disguise . . . she wore no makeup! However, even when she wasn't working, Dolly couldn't stop being creative. On one three-week "vacation," Dolly wrote thirty-seven songs!

In 1999, Dolly was inducted into the Country Music Hall of Fame. Usually, the award is given

COUNTRY MUSIC HALL OF FAME

to people at the end of their career, but not Dolly! She was only fifty-six, and she was just getting rolling! In her acceptance speech Dolly joked, "I thought you had to be ugly or dead to get in."

Sadly, a short time later, Dolly's father, Lee, died at age seventy-nine. She said he was the "best daddy a bunch of kids could ever have." Dolly dedicated an album to him, *Little Sparrow*. Only three years later, Dolly's mom, Avie Lee, died and was buried next to Lee. How wonderful that her parents lived long enough to see Dolly's big dreams come true.

Far more than a popular performer, Dolly has come to be valued as a national treasure. In 2004 Dolly received her second Living Legend award, a medal from the US Library of Congress. It honors people who have made America a better place, like children's book author Maurice Sendak, astronaut Sally Ride, General Colin Powell, cellist Yo-Yo Ma, and entertainer Bill Cosby.

Then in 2005, Dolly was invited to the White House, where President George W. Bush would present her with the National Medal of Arts. In the United States, it's the highest award an artist can receive. But

Dolly had to pick up her award later . . . she was doing a concert in Oklahoma and, as always, performing for her fans came first.

HOW DOLLY MAKES AN ALBUM

FOR A NEW ALBUM, DOLLY MAY COME INTO THE RECORDING STUDIO WITH ABOUT TWENTY-FIVE NEW SONGS. SHE WILL SING AND PLAY THEM ON GUITAR. WITH THE HELP OF PEOPLE IN THE STUDIO, SHE NARROWS THE NUMBER OF SONGS DOWN TO TWELVE OR SO. A PRODUCER THEN WRITES OUT THE SONGS FOR THE STUDIO MUSICIANS. DOLLY WILL SING FOR THEM SO THEY GET THE IDEA OF WHAT SHE WANTS. THEN THE MUSICIANS ADD THEIR OWN IDEAS AND REHEARSE FOR ABOUT A WEEK. FINALLY, DOLLY AND THE MUSICIANS ARE ABLE TO RECORD TOGETHER . . . SOMETIMES TWO SONGS IN A DAY. MAKING AN ALBUM DOESN'T HAPPEN OVERNIGHT!

Chapter 10
Still Dreaming

From the beginning, Dolly Parton wanted to perform live for a crowd. The joy of sharing her music has never left her. She says, "it's a lovefest with me and my audience." Her fans give her energy. She has toured almost every year since 2002. In 2011, she had a very successful tour in Australia. You might wonder why people halfway around the world from Tennessee would be so crazy for a country-music star. Dolly's honest personality and her songs are universal. Everybody experiences the same kinds of joy and pain in life.

Dolly is still recording, writing, touring, and appearing on TV. Recently she published a book, *Dream More,* where she shares her thoughts about life. She still looks glitzy, but is as down-to-earth as ever. No one works harder, and no one has more fun. She has a million ideas and always keeps a pencil and paper handy to write them down. Dolly Parton is still dreaming big.

What are her dreams now? She says she wants

to write more books and do music for children. She wants to write a Broadway musical based on her life. She wants to own her own cosmetics company. And more!

In her late sixties, she still has the energy of ten people. Dolly says, "The older I get, the earlier I get up." She won't stop working. It's what she loves. Her wish is to keep performing and die in the middle of a song on stage with a smile on her face . . . at age one-hundred and twenty!

Dolly Parton has made a lot of money and given away a lot of money. Famous around the world, she never has strayed from her roots. On the lawn in front of the courthouse in Sevierville, Tennessee, there is a life-size bronze statue of her. It was put there by the people who knew her best. The statue is of young barefoot Dolly in rolled-up jeans sitting on a rock with her guitar . . . dreaming.

TIMELINE OF
DOLLY PARTON'S LIFE

1946	Born January 19 in Sevier County, Tennessee
1956	First radio appearance
1964	Graduates from Sevierville High School; goes to Nashville
1966	Records with Monument Records; marries Carl Dean
1967	First appears on *The Porter Wagoner Show*
1969	Becomes a member of the Grand Ole Opry
1971	"Joshua" and "Coat of Many Colors" are hits
1973	"Jolene" is a hit
1974	Ends working with Porter. CMA Artist of the Year; "I Will Always Love You" is a hit
1977	New band: Gypsy Fever
1978	Is awarded CMA Entertainer of the Year
1980	Movie *Nine to Five* opens
1986	Dollywood opens
1987	*Trio* with Ronstadt and Harris wins Grammy award
1988	Founds Dollywood Foundation
1989	Movie *Steel Magnolias* opens
1994	Receives first Living Legend award from the US Library of Congress
1999	Is inducted into CMA Hall of Fame
2004	Receives second Living Legend award
2005	Receives National Medal of Arts
2009	Receives honorary doctorate from The University of Tennessee
2012	Publishes *Dream More*
2013	The Imagination Library gives away its fifty millionth book

TIMELINE OF THE WORLD

World War II begins	1939
World War II ends	1945
George Orwell's *1984* is published	1949
Patsy Cline begins recording for Four Star Records	1955
Elvis records his hit "Heartbreak Hotel"	1956
Rock and roll musicians Buddy Holly, Richie Valens, and J. P. "The Big Bopper" Richards are killed in a plane crash Barbie doll is introduced	1959
US President John F. Kennedy is shot and killed	1963
Beatlemania hits the United States	1964
A huge protest takes place against the Vietnam War in Washington, DC	1967
Neil Armstrong becomes the first man to walk on the moon The Woodstock music festival takes place in August in upstate New York	1969
President Richard Nixon resigns	1974
Margaret Thatcher becomes the first woman prime minister of Great Britain	1979
John Lennon is shot dead in New York City	1980
MTV starts broadcasting rock music videos	1981
The first House of Blues opens	1993
On September 11, terrorists attack the Twin Towers in New York City and the Pentagon in Washington, DC	2001
The Iraq War begins	2003
Barack Obama becomes the first African American president of the United States	2009
The Iraq War ends	2011

BIBLIOGRAPHY

Miller, Stephen. **Smart Blonde: Dolly Parton**. Omnibus, London, 2008.

Parton, Dolly. **Coat of Many Colors**. Illustrated by Judith Sutton. Harper Collins, New York, 1994.

Parton, Dolly. **Dream More! Celebrate the Dreamer in You**. G.P. Putnam, 2012.

Parton, Dolly. **Dolly, My Life and Other Unfinished Business**. New York: Harper Collins, 1994.

Parton, Dolly. **I Am A Rainbow**. Illustrated by Heather Sheffield. Puffin, New York, 2009.

Parton, Willadeene. **In the Shadow of a Song**. Bantam, New York, 1985.

WEBSITES

dollypartonmusic.net

dollymania.net

dollyon-line.com

imaginationlibrary.com

facebook.com/Dolly Parton